The Little Book

Professor Richard Wiseman has carried out extensive research into the psychology of luck and has featured on hundreds of radio and television programmes to present his findings. Articles about his work have appeared in *The Times*, the *Daily Telegraph* and the *Guardian*. He is also the author of the top-ten bestseller *The Luck Factor* and *Did You Spot the Gorilla?*

ALSO BY RICHARD WISEMAN

The Luck Factor
Did You Spot the Gorilla?

THE
LITTLE BOOK
OF
LUCK

Richard Wiseman

arrow books

Published in the United Kingdom in 2004 by Arrow Books

3 5 7 9 10 8 6 4 2

Copyright © Richard Wiseman, 2004

The right of Richard Wiseman to be identified as the author of this work has been asserted by him in accordance with the Copyright, Designs and Patents Act, 1988

Arrow Books
The Random House Group Limited
20 Vauxhall Bridge Road, London SW1V 2SA

Random House Australia (Pty) Limited
20 Alfred Street, Milsons Point, Sydney, New South Wales 2061, Australia

Random House New Zealand Limited
18 Poland Road, Glenfield, Auckland 10, New Zealand

Random House (Pty) Limited
Isle of Houghton, Corner of Boundary Road & Carse O'Gowrie,
Houghton 2198, South Africa

The Random House Group Limited Reg. No. 954009
www.randomhouse.co.uk

A CIP catalogue record for this book is available from the British Library

Papers used by Random House are natural, recyclable products made from wood grown in sustainable forests. The manufacturing processes conform to the environmental regulations of the country of origin

Typeset in Carolina, Minion and Rotis

Design and make up by Roger Walker

Printed and bound in the United Kingdom by
Cox & Wyman Ltd, Reading, Berkshire

ISBN 0 09 944328 7

Introduction

Luck exerts a dramatic influence over our lives.

A few seconds of bad fortune can unravel years of striving, while a moment of good luck can lead to success and happiness.

Luck has the power to transform the improbable into the possible; to make the difference between life and death, reward and ruin, happiness and despair.

But why are some people exceptionally lucky while others encounter little but ill fortune?

For the past ten years I have carried out scientific research into luck, examining the lives of hundreds of lucky and unlucky people.

This work has revealed that lucky and unlucky people create much of their good and bad fortune by the way they think and behave.

More importantly, my research has shown that everyone has the potential to increase their luck.

The Little Book of Luck

Unlucky people can become lucky and lucky people can become even luckier.

The Little Book of Luck is based on this work and will help you live a lucky life.

It is a bite-sized, fact-packed, fun guide that is full of top tips, practical exercises and inspirational quotes designed to help you increase your luck.

Have fun and be lucky.

RICHARD WISEMAN

'An ounce of
luck is better
than a pound
of wisdom. '

ITALIAN PROVERB

The Little Book of Luck

The power of the new

Lucky people love new experiences.

Bring good fortune into your life with this simple exercise that is guaranteed to induce novelty and fun.

Simply think of two new experiences that you wouldn't mind trying. Keep your choices realistic and safe. For example, you might decide to buy a very unusual piece of clothing, go to see a film that you think you won't enjoy, try a new type of food, travel to work via a new and unusual route, go to watch a professional wrestling match, visit the park and feed the ducks, stay in bed all day, visit the zoo, sign-up for a course on clowning, learn to say hello in six different languages, discover how to draw cartoons, go to a museum or art gallery that you haven't been to before, learn how to make a really good cup of coffee, go parachuting or donate some of your time to charity work.

Write both of the experiences down and label one 'heads' and the other 'tails'.

Next, randomly choose one of the two experiences by flipping a coin.

Now comes the really important bit.

The Little Book of Luck

Do not back out of the experience.

Instead, simply go and do it.

Many people are surprised at the odd coincidences and lucky breaks that flow from their new experiences. They meet new people, and new opportunities present themselves.

Repeat the exercise every few weeks, thinking of your own new experiences, and feel the luck flood into your life.

Be daring.

Be random.

Be lucky.

The Little Book of Luck

Luck school

For the past few years I have carried out a series of experiments called 'luck school'.

I wanted to discover whether people could become luckier by thinking and behaving like a lucky person, and so I asked hundreds of people to incorporate the exercises described in this book into their lives.

The results have been amazing. Over 80 per cent of people have reported an increase in their luck, and many have transformed their entire lives.

I have included some of their stories to demonstrate both the power of the exercises, and the benefits that can flow from thinking and behaving like a lucky person.

The first account describes how creating opportunities and new experiences in your life can help you become lucky in love.

I've always been unlucky in love. As part of 'luck school' I decided to make a real effort to change. I noticed that my local newspaper ran a dating column and I placed a small advert.

I also felt that I was in a rut, so to introduce something new I decided to fulfil one of my ambitions and learn how to rock-climb.

In my newspaper ad, I mentioned that I was about to learn rock-climbing, and a few weeks later a really nice guy contacted me because he had also always wanted to try rock-climbing.

We have now been dating for eight months and I think my search for my perfect man is finally over!

Tina, 36, personal assistant

The Little Book of Luck

"No one is luckier than the person who believes in his luck. "

GERMAN PROVERB

I am lucky because . . .

In a moment I am going to ask you to complete five sentences.

Each one will begin with the words 'I am lucky because . . .'.

You can give any type of answer you like.

Some of your answers could refer to aspects of your life that you often take for granted, such having easy access to clean drinking water or a warm place to sleep at night. Others could refer to very specific aspects of your life, such as being lucky because you know a certain person or have a job that you enjoy or have achieved a childhood ambition.

OK, please turn the page and complete the five sentences.

1 I am lucky because_____

_____

2 I am lucky because_____

_____

3 I am lucky because_____

_____

4 I am lucky because_____

_____

5 I am lucky because_____

_____

Lucky people have a strong sense of gratitude and focus on what has worked out well in their lives.

Look back at the list you have just made and remember how lucky you really are.

The secret of a lucky life is . . .

I recently asked one thousand lucky people to complete the sentence 'The secret of a lucky life is . . .'

I have scattered some of the more popular, interesting, unusual, insightful and fun answers throughout the book.

Here is the first one . . .

The secret of a lucky life is being grateful for what you already have.

Erica, 45, television producer

"Behind bad luck comes good.

ROMANY PROVERB

The Little Book of Luck

A blessing in disguise

Everyone experiences bad fortune at some point during their lives. However, these seemingly unlucky events often have an uncanny way of working out for the best in the long run. When bad things happen, spend a few moments thinking about how the event might be a blessing in disguise, and how you can make good luck flow from your apparent ill fortune.

When a lucky person fails a job interview, they might think, 'Well, maybe it was meant to be – after all, it means that I am still in the job market and so perhaps I will now find an even better position, one that I would have missed if I had been offered the first job.' And when they are unlucky enough to have an accident, they might use the event to help re-evaluate their life and realise the importance of the things that really matter, such as their family and friends.

You cannot change the bad luck that has happened to you, but you can control how you respond to your apparent ill fortune.

Treat bad luck as a blessing in disguise.

Each misfortune you encounter will carry in it the seed of tomorrow's good luck.

OG MANDINO,
author of *The Greatest Salesman in the World*

Every wall is a door.

RALPH WALDO EMERSON,
American author, poet and philosopher

The Little Book of Luck

The secret of a lucky
life is to always open
a packet of crisps the
right way up.

Marcus, 33, engineer

Should I . . . ?

Are you trying to make an important decision and simply cannot decide what to do? Perhaps you are thinking about changing jobs or starting a new relationship or emigrating to another country.

Write the question that is on your mind in the space below, making sure that it is phrased in such a way that it can be answered with a simple yes or no:

Should I _____

The next page has two circles on it.

Without thinking about it, simply turn
the page and quickly place the first
finger of your right hand into one of
the circles.

Do it now.

The Little Book of Luck

Perhaps the circle that you chose was not as random as you might think.

Maybe you were guided by your unconscious.

Perhaps your intuition is trying to tell you something.

Maybe you have just found the answer to your question.

Lucky people tend to trust their intuition and lucky hunches – do you?

Decisions, decisions

Lucky people do not see their decisions in life as being right and wrong. As one lucky person explained to me:

'I don't believe that you can ever know if any decision you made was for the best. After all, you never know what life would have been like if you had made the opposite decision. To me, the big mistake is to be indecisive – the important thing is to make a decision, and then work away at making a success of the situation. Don't agonise about trying to make the right decision. Make the decision and then make the best of it.'

The secret of a lucky life is smoked salmon, strawberries and white-water rafting.

Anne, 57, grandmother

Treat yourself

Unlucky people are often very hard on themselves. They slave away, day after day, but take little pleasure in what they do. Lucky people are the opposite. They work hard, but they also take time off to enjoy life's little pleasures. It might be something as simple as a good cup of coffee or taking a long bath. Or it might involve spending an entire day doing exactly what they want to do, when they want to do it.

Why not treat yourself tomorrow? What are you going to do and when are you going to do it?

The secret of a lucky life is doing anything with wonderful people.

Richard, 40, farmer

Building your 'network of luck'

Lucky people enjoy being with others, and the more people they meet, the greater the chances of them having a lucky encounter that will change their life.

Here are five top tips for boosting your network of luck:

1 Telephone a friend who you haven't seen for some time and find out what is happening in their life.

2 Make the time to be at that party that you didn't think you had time to go to.

3 Find something that really interests you and seek out others interested in the same thing.

4 Say hi instead of rushing on.

5 Sign up for an evening class.

Remember, just one lucky encounter can change your whole life. The more people you meet, the more likely you are to have that lucky encounter.

'One chance is all you need. '

JESSE OWENS,
athlete and Olympic champion 1936

The Little Book of Luck

Your declaration

Let me ask you a question.

Are you really open to the idea of increasing your luck by changing the way you think and behave?

If so, you will have to be prepared to invest some time and effort into the process.

To help create the necessary sense of commitment, I often ask people to look at the declaration on the following page.

'I want to increase my luck, and, for the next two weeks, am prepared to try to make the necessary changes in the way that I think and behave.'

If you are serious about wanting to increase your luck, please copy this declaration on to the next page and sign your name underneath.

My declaration:

_____

_____

_____

_____

Signed:

_____

Date:

_____

Thank you.

Now let me ask you a second question.

Are you the sort of person who breaks promises?

You have just made a promise to yourself – how are you going to fulfil it?

You only have two weeks – and your time starts right now. Each week, choose two of the exercises from the book and start to experience more good fortune.

The secret of a lucky life is watermelon lipgloss!

Karla, 32, mum of Brendan

Affirmations

Lucky people are very positive about the future, and these expectations help transform their dreams into reality.

To help convince yourself that your future will be bright and lucky, say the following affirmation out loud each morning for a week:

'I am a lucky person and today is going to be another lucky day.'

The Little Book of Luck

Being positive about the future has really helped. I had to force myself to start the day saying the affirmations, but after a while it became more subconscious and automatic.

Both my boyfriend and parents have definitely noticed a change. I now feel far more positive about the future, which is amazing, because to make me positive is a real achievement. It's definitely had an amazing effect. I simply don't think of myself as being particularly unlucky any more.

Patricia, 28, cabin crew

The secret of a lucky
life is good coffee,
Sunday papers and
family sounds
around the house.

Carole, 45, mother of five

The Little Book of Luck

Set lucky goals

Lucky people set goals for themselves, and this helps them notice opportunities that bring these goals closer.

Use the following page to list two short-term goals for the next month and two medium-term goals for the next six months.

Make your goals both specific and achievable. Review the list on a regular basis and watch your goals become reality.

Short-term goals:

1 _____

_____

2 _____

_____

Medium-term goals:

1 _____

_____

2 _____

_____

The secret of a lucky
life is to remember
that we are all in it
together.

Ronald, 70, retired engineer

Win-win

Lucky people are out to make long-term relationships, in both their personal and their professional lives. They want people to have a good time with them, and so be eager to come back for more.

They realise that we are all living in the same small world and they invest energy in trying to create win-win situations rather than just thinking about themselves.

Increase your own luck by helping others be lucky.

" Charms have not their power from contracts with spirits, but proceed wholly from strengthening the imagination. "

SIR FRANCIS BACON,
Renaissance author and courtier

Works like a charm

Lucky charms have existed in every culture throughout time and they are still very popular today.

A few years ago I carried out an experiment to scientifically test the effects of carrying a luck charm.

One hundred people were asked to carry a lucky Victorian penny for just over a month, and to use it to remind themselves to 'think lucky'.

The results revealed that the charms provided an amazing psychological benefit.

The penny provided people with an increased sense of security and made them more positive about the future. The charms made them think like a lucky person and over 30 per cent reported that their luck had improved.

Interestingly, at the end of the study 70 per cent of participants said that they would continue to carry the charm!

Carry a charm

It could be a lucky coin, a gemstone or even just a pebble.

Whatever it is, slip it into your pocket or place it somewhere you will see it every day and let it remind you to be open, happy, opportunistic, optimistic and lucky.

The Little Book of Luck

My luck was down to begin with, then it picked up after I started carrying the penny. It came to represent a symbolic change in luck for me. I thought of it as being instrumental in helping me to change my attitude. I put it in my pocket and whenever I touched it, or saw it, I was reminded that I could create my own destiny. A few weeks later, I was contacted by a potential employer, and a few weeks after that I was offered a new job. Was it all down to the coin? I have no idea, but I am certainly holding on to the penny!

Jonathan, 36, participant in the lucky-charm experiment

The secret of a lucky life is knowing how to mix a mean G & T.

Elizabeth, 55, artist

The Little Book of Luck

Take responsibility

Lucky people take responsibility for their own failings.

Rather than blame bad luck, they learn from the past and make sure that they do not make the same mistakes.

Are you blaming bad luck when you really need to take responsibility?

The secret of a lucky life is not to burn your bridges, no matter how rickety they may seem.

Sarah, arts manager

The Little Book of Luck

Your luck diary

Lucky people focus on the aspects of
their lives that are positive and
successful. To help you think like a
lucky person, try keeping a luck diary.

For the next four days use the following
pages to make a note of as many lucky
events as possible. Include events that
seem relatively trivial as well as those
that are more important.

Each morning, flick through your luck
diary to remind yourself of the good
things that have happened to you on
the previous days.

Day 1

Here are a few of the lucky things that
have happened to me today . . .

_____

_____

_____

_____

_____

_____

_____

_____

The Little Book of Luck

Day 2

Here are a few of the lucky things that
have happened to me today . . .

_____

_____

_____

_____

_____

_____

_____

_____

Day 3

Here are a few of the lucky things that
have happened to me today . . .

_____

_____

_____

_____

_____

_____

_____

_____

_____

Day 4

Here are a few of the lucky things that
have happened to me today . . .

_____

_____

_____

_____

_____

_____

_____

_____

How do you feel now?

Creating a lucky life will take time.

Be patient and enjoy the process.

One step at a time.

Each change you make, and each piece of good luck you encounter, no matter how tiny, is a step in the right direction.

And even the longest of journeys is made up of many small steps.

The Little Book of Luck

Keeping the luck diary made me think completely differently. It made me open my eyes and think, 'Wow – good things do happen to me after all.'

And as time was going on, more and more good things were happening and fewer and fewer bad things.

It started to have a real effect then. It was just small things at first, but that made me feel more positive about life, and it started to seep in.

Patricia, 28, cabin crew

The secret of a lucky life is cheap underwear, but plenty of it.

Lalitavira, 39, storyteller

The Little Book of Luck

The power of passion

Lucky people follow their passion in life. We all have hidden ambitions and secret dreams, but often convince ourselves that these will never become reality.

Yet the barriers that we construct are often little more than an illusion. Lucky people sweep aside these self-imposed constraints and enjoy the good fortune and energy that flow from following their passion.

What is your real passion in life? And how are you going to make it happen?

I recently decided to try to change my luck – I spent some time thinking about what made me feel happy, and remembered that one of my youthful ambitions was to work with tigers.

Everyone said that it was impossible for me to fulfil my dream, but I decided to give it a try. I contacted a national tiger sanctuary, explaining my childhood interest and offering to spend some time helping out. I recently received an invitation to do just that, and boy did my heart soar. I feel the luckiest person in the world!

Sammy, 47, accountant

The Little Book of Luck

Make the decision, then stop

Facing an important question in your life?

To find out how you really feel about your options, simply choose one of them and commit your decision to paper.

If, for example, you are uncertain about whether to quit your job, just write your resignation letter.

Now stop.

How do you feel?

Do you really want to send that letter or is there something inside telling you that it doesn't feel right? Is that your intuition or are you simply afraid of change? When it came to the crunch, what did your inner voice say to you?

Lucky people use their intuition as an alarm bell – a good reason to stop and consider the situation carefully.

How about you?

Persevere

Lucky people are prepared to persevere, even in the face of great adversity.

Think like them.

Be open to the idea of taking a break, or trying a different way of achieving your goals, but be prepared to try, and try and try again, until your dreams and ambitions come true.

' All of us have bad luck and good luck. The man who persists through the bad luck, who keeps right on going, is the man who is there when the good luck comes – and is ready to receive it. '

ROBERT COLLIER,
author of *The Secret of the Ages*

The Little Book of Luck

I was made redundant and finding it very hard to find a job. A couple of weeks ago I received two rejections and was at my lowest point ever. Then I decided, 'NO, it's not going to be bad,' so I sat down at my computer and went through the jobs pages again.

I saw a position I knew I would enjoy. I then did some research and contacted the Chairman directly. I received a reply within 48 hours and then the offer of an interview. The interview went well and I was offered the position.

Thinking lucky has had such a positive effect on me that my boyfriend is actually starting to feel my attitude and luck rubbing off on him!

Jessica, 39, sales representative

> " I am a great believer in luck, and I find the harder I work, the more I have of it. "

THOMAS JEFFERSON,
third President of the United States

Become a social magnet

Lucky people have a kind of 'social magnetism' that draws other people to them.

Improve your social magnetism using the following tips:

❶ Find something you really like and respect about someone and tell them.

❷ In meetings and at parties uncross your arms and legs, smile and keep your hands away from your face.

The Little Book of Luck

3 Maintain friendly amounts of eye contact. Just enough to discover the colour of their eyes but not so much that they start to think you are odd.

4 Be genuinely interested in others, and talk about them not you.

5 Look for something you find really interesting and tell other people about it.

6 Stop complaining about your bad luck. No one likes to be around someone who is always complaining – be positive.

The secret of a lucky life is always to smile at everyone.

Miranda, 40, housewife

The Little Book of Luck

Smile your way to good fortune

Your face is amazing. It is made up of twenty-two pairs of muscles that animate your skin, creating a constantly changing mask capable of displaying over ten thousand expressions.

But only one of these expressions is instantly recognisable in every culture, and has the power to make you, and the people around you, instantly feel happy and lucky.

Your smile.

Research shows that lucky people smile 37.567 per cent more often than unlucky people.

Try it. Right now. Force your face into a smile.

Now your mission for the rest of the day is to get others to wear the same expression on their face.

The smiling wizard

In the 1920s, Howard Thurston was the most famous magician in America and had an incredible reputation for being a highly charismatic performer.

When asked how he achieved this amazing effect, Thurston explained that a few moments before walking out on stage he thought about how grateful he was that the audience had made the effort to come to his show, and how they allowed him to live his life in a very agreeable way. Once those thoughts had seeped in, he gave the signal for the curtain to go up, and walked out on stage with a warm, genuine smile on his face.

Just before a meeting a friend, spend a few moments thinking about the difference that this person makes to your life. Before a business meeting, reflect upon how the meeting could transform your life.

Like Thurston, let these thoughts seep into your mind and put a genuine smile on your face.

Now, like Thurston, go out and perform the impossible.

Never frown, because you never know when someone is falling in love with your smile.

ANON.

‘Start every day off with a smile and get it over with.’

W. C. FIELDS,
American comedian and actor

See the funny side

Lucky people have a good sense of humour. They find life funny and this helps soften the emotional impact of ill fortune.

Trying to get through life without a sense of humour is like driving along a bumpy road with bad suspension – you are shaken by all of the bumps and holes.

Learn to laugh and find the funny side of bad luck.

"I am so unlucky – last night I peeled a banana and it was empty."

ANON.

Be constructive

Lucky people approach the problems in their lives in constructive ways. They think through new and creative ways of tackling the bad luck that has happened.

Top tips for being constructive:

1 Take control of the situation.

2 Think through as many different options as possible.

3 Decide on how you are going to move forward.

4 Most important of all, start to solve the problem.

Give up fixating on the problem and do what lucky people do – concentrate on taking control and finding a solution.

I have always regarded myself as a very unlucky person. I was unhappy with my job and had been looking for a new one without success. I had sent a few letters to people but heard nothing back, so felt very dejected. During luck school I decided to be more positive. I contacted one of the companies again and asked for feedback. They said my letter came across as hesitant and I was applying for jobs that simply didn't match my qualifications. It was as if I was almost creating the bad luck myself by setting totally unrealistic goals. I decided to have another go but this time I sent letters to larger companies and emphasised my core skills. Two days later, I was invited for an interview. The job was far from perfect and I almost declined the offer. Then I thought how lucky people are always out to maximise their opportunities, so I decided to go along. I went for the interview and talked frankly about myself. That afternoon the company called and asked to see me again. I went in and they said that they were so impressed by my attitude that they had decided to change the role and offer me a more senior position.

From letter to job offer in just 4 days!

Chris, 34, surveyor

The Little Book of Luck

"When good luck comes to you, invite her in.

SPANISH PROVERB

Learning how to be lucky has made me feel a lot more in control. I am a master of what happens to me.

When my car broke down before, the first thing on my mind would have been, 'It always happens to me, it never happens to anybody else.' And now it's, 'All right, well, how am I going to deal with it now?'

So it's far more positive and constructive.

Louise, 23, student

The secret of a lucky life is not being afraid to wear red shoes.

Lucy, 37, research psychologist
and red shoe wearer

Do not dwell on ill fortune

Lucky people do not focus on the bad luck they encounter.

Top tips for moving on:

1 Exercise – take a brisk walk or go to the gym.

2 Watch a funny film.

3 Write down a happy event from your past and relive the event in your mind.

4 Listen to some music that always puts you in a good mood.

5 Arrange to see your friends and talk about what's happening in their lives.

Remember that you cannot alter the past. What has happened has happened and that is that. However, you can move on. Put the past behind you and focus on what has yet to be.

' Luck is believing you're lucky. '

TENNESSEE WILLIAMS,
American playwright

The Little Book of Luck

Opportunity knocks

Lucky people are relaxed about life and therefore notice opportunities that others miss.

Top tips for spotting opportunities:

1 Slow down and enjoy the moment.

2 Do not focus on just one goal and a rigid way of achieving that goal. Be more fluid and open to chance.

3 Be playful and have fun.

❹ Do not let opportunity pass you by
– seize the moment.

❺ Do not become entangled in the
small stuff – step back and see the
bigger picture.

Seeing an opportunity is one thing, but
making the most of what you have seen
is another.

Find the courage to make the most of
the opportunities that will come your
way.

"Luck is when opportunity knocks and you answer. "

ANON.

A few weeks ago I was walking back to my car in the garage and I saw a piece of paper on the ground. Normally I would have walked past it, but instead I treated it as an opportunity! I kicked it and there was a £20 note underneath. And when I picked it up I realised it was five £20 notes – £100 in cash. It was just lying there.

Joseph, 35, mature student

The Little Book of Luck

'Four things never come back: the spoken word, the spent arrow, the past and the neglected opportunity.'

OMAR IDN AL-HALIF,
Arab scholar

I tried the luck-school exercises and not only has my perception of myself as a lucky person increased, my actual 'objective' luck increased. I would miss the bus only to run into a friend who was taking a cab in the same direction as I was going and ask if I would like a free ride? And so on. More and more these fortunate unplanned coincidences popped up in my life. At the end of the month it felt like smooth sailing. I was very sceptical, but it does actually seem to work.

Brian, 46, journalist

The secret of a lucky
life is to always be
curious.

William, 64, retired airline pilot

> "The very best thing in all this world that can befall a man is to be born lucky."

MARK TWAIN,
American writer and humourist

The Little Book of Luck

Born lucky?

As part of the Edinburgh International Science Festival I carried out a large experiment to investigate whether some people are born lucky.

Over forty thousand people submitted their date of birth and rated the degree to which they were lucky.

The results revealed that summer-borns (March–August) considered themselves luckier and more optimistic than winter-borns (September–February).

Fifty per cent of people born in May considered themselves lucky, making it the luckiest month.

However, winter-borns shouldn't feel too down about the result – the effect is very small and remember, people can improve their luck.

Summer-borns include . . .

. . . rugby player Jonny Wilkinson (May)

. . . author J. K. Rowling (July)

. . . footballer David Beckham (May)

. . . model Jordan (May).

The secret of a lucky life is to never follow the crowd.

Danny, 24, marketing consultant

Looking on the positive side

Lucky people tend to see the positive side of their ill fortune. They imagine how things could have been worse. If they fall down the stairs and twist their ankle they believe that they are really lucky, because they could have broken their neck.

Whenever ill fortune strikes, think like a lucky person and look on the bright side. You may have experienced a car accident, but at least you survived. You may have been late for an important appointment, but there again, you could have missed it altogether.

The Little Book of Luck

"Failure is only the opportunity to begin again, only this time more wisely.

ANON.

Choose your comparisons wisely

There will always be people who have more than you. People with more money, more good looks, more talent, more opportunities and so on. If you always compare yourself to such people, you will always feel unlucky.

Instead, do what lucky people do – be grateful for what you have and remember that there are many people who have far less than you.

The secret of a lucky life is always to carry a double-headed coin.

John, 32, writer

Does it really matter?

Lucky people do not get dragged down by life's daily grind because they put things in perspective.

You may have been turned down for a promotion, but will that affect the important aspects of your life, such as your health and your relationships with others? You may have lost your wallet and credit cards, but does that really matter in the overall scheme of your life?

When ill fortune strikes, ask yourself one question: 'Does it *really* matter?'

Luck school definitely made a difference, because bad luck doesn't drag me down now. Unlucky things still happen – for example, my television has just stopped working – but I don't seem to notice these sorts of little things any more. In the past I'd miss the bus, and then something else would happen, and then there would be a pile of unlucky events, and I'd get really fed up. But now, if I miss the bus I can think through how it's not a really an issue, how it doesn't really matter compared to the important things in my life. I just don't even think about it.

Jane, 26, events organiser

The secret of a lucky life is making the most of a bad moment.

Tom, 60, retired compositor

The Little Book of Luck

Your 'inner voice'

Lucky people listen to their intuition and use it as an alarm bell – a good reason to stop and consider the situation carefully.

When you are faced with a decision, spend a few moments forgetting about logic and reason, what others think you should do, or what you think you should do out of a sense of duty. Instead, simply focus on how you feel about each of the options. Be totally honest. If you felt uneasy about an option, even though the evidence suggests that it is correct, then it is perhaps best to reconsider.

The secret of a lucky life is doing most things for a purpose, but quite a lot of things just for the hell of it.

Sarah, 36, management consultant

"The pessimist sees difficulty in every opportunity. The optimist sees the opportunity in every difficulty."

WINSTON CHURCHILL,
British Prime Minister

Expect to be lucky

Lucky people have high expectations about their interactions and relationships with others. In both their personal and professional lives, they expect the people around them to be interesting, productive and fun.

Think through telephone calls and meetings before they happen, and imagine how the people involved will be positive towards you.

Expect the best out of the people around you – you might be surprised at the effect that it has on your life.

The Little Book of Luck

Make your own luck

To help remind you of the importance
of being positive, cut out the panel on
the next page and place it where you
will see it every morning.

Make
Today
Lucky

The Little Book of Luck

Visualise good fortune

Whenever you are faced with an important situation, spend a few moments beforehand imagining yourself being lucky and successful. If you are going for a job interview, think about the types of questions that are likely to arise and imagine yourself giving great answers. If you are thinking about a date, imagine yourself being confident and relaxed. Have fun by trying to see the situation from their point of view and then shifting back to your viewpoint.

Focus on being lucky and then make your expectations a reality.

Luck school has been wonderful, much better than I expected. I've had an excellent time. I always had a lucky outlook, but it is especially positive now. Other people have noticed some kind of change. They have become more positive with me.

Joseph, 35, mature student

The Little Book of Luck

The secret of a lucky life is not getting found out.

Richard, 58, bridge player

Throw a lucky man in the sea and he will come up with a fish in his mouth.

ARAB PROVERB

The Little Book of Luck

Shape your destiny

Your future isn't set in stone.

You can change.

You can create far more lucky breaks and massively increase how often you are in the right place at the right time.

You can create your own destiny.

When it comes to luck, the future is in your hands.

And it starts right now.

Go and wake up your luck.

PERSIAN PROVERB

The Little Book of Luck